The Concise Adair on Creativity and Innovation

Edited by Neil Thomas

THOROGOOD

Published by Thorogood Publishing Ltd
10–12 Rivington Street
London EC2A 3DU

Telephone: 020 7749 4748
Fax: 020 7729 6110
Email: info@thorogood.ws
Web: www.thorogood.ws

A CIP catalogue record for this book is
available from the British Library.

ISBN 1 85418 273 0

Typeset by Bookens Ltd, Royston, Herts

Printed in India by Replika Press Pvt.Ltd.

The author and editor

John Adair

John Adair is internationally acknowledged as having had a significant influence on management and leadership development in both the business and military spheres. He has seen military service, lectured at Sandhurst, worked extensively as a consultant, held professorships in Leadership Studies and authored well received management and leadership books, including *Inspiring Leadership, The Adair Handbook of Management and Leadership, The Concise Adair on Leadership, The Concise Time Management and Personal Development* and *The Concise Adair on Communication and Presentation Skills*. (www.johnadair.co.uk)

Neil Thomas

Neil Thomas is the Chairman of Thorogood Publishing Ltd and Managing Director of Falconbury Ltd. He has been involved in publishing and seminar/training for over twenty-five years. (www.thorogood.ws, www.falconbury.co.uk)

Contents

Introduction

New ideas are essential for industry, they are the lifeblood of successful organisations. Creative and innovative thinking, the means by which ideas are born and nurtured, are not products of clearly defined steps, they can be encouraged in various ways.

We all have new ideas but really good, creative new ideas vary in quality and frequency. A good idea can be classed as one that a critical mass of people consider to be both useful and original. Those people who have a high rate of excellent ideas are the true creative thinkers. Most creative thinkers can be placed on a scale relative to their quality and quantity of ideas.

High	A High productivity and few quality ideas	C Many quality ideas in high quality
	B Not very productive and not producing many 'pearls'	D Many quality ideas with low productivity
Low	QUALITY OF IDEAS	High

Really good managers (and all successful businesses have them) are capable of having, or recognising, good ideas and using them to make things happen in a new way: of translating ideas into useful, practicable and commercial products, services or systems.

Innovation (to bring in or introduce something new – a new idea, method or device) draws together new ideas *and* their implementation, whereas creativity is the having of new ideas which, in an organisation, are generated or spotted by individuals or teams.

It is important for all managers and leaders to:
- understand creativity and the creative processes
- eliminate impediments to creativity and creative thinking
- widen their field of view as well as that of their staff
- build on ideas and not merely criticise them
- tolerate doubts and uncertainties
- adopt a creative attitude in listening, observing and reading
- be confident in your own creative skills
- make time to think
- participate creatively as a leader, manager or member of a team
- use teams to innovate effectively
- manage innovation in your business.

How far you develop your and your teams' creative abilities is largely up to you. Your motivation to succeed will dictate how far you exert yourself to learn all you can about the art of being creative and innovative. Personal experience is a great way to learn once you understand the basic principles and thought processes.

Use the principles set out in this book to build your mind and encourage the right mind set to become more creative and innovative. The benefits this book can bring to you include:

- Developing your understanding of the creative process
- Overcoming the barriers to having new ideas and creative thoughts
- Enlarging your parameters of vision and information
- Building on your ideas as well as criticising them when relevant
- Increasing your tolerance for uncertainty and doubt
- Reading, listening and absorbing information around you with a creative mind
- Making you aware of having time to think
- Giving you confidence in yourself to be creative
- Encouraging you to be a more effective manager or leader to build creative teams
- Managing innovation within your organisation for the most successful outcomes.

Remember, the future of our civilisation depends on the creative flair and innovative genius of people like you.

This book is divided into two parts: **Part one: creative thinking** looks at obstacles to creativity and ways to improve it personally and organisationally; and **Part two: innovation** details how best to manage creativity and encourage innovation successfully in business.

Creative thinking

Part one: Creative thinking

The creative process

Creativity can be improved by remembering that the creative process has four main stages and each needs to be properly 'worked':

1 **Preparation:** information gathering, analysis and solution exploration.
2 **Incubation:** letting the mind work to continue the process sub-consciously.
3 **Illumination:** inspiration – which can come when the individual is not necessarily thinking about the problem but is in a relaxed frame of mind.
4 **Verification:** testing ideas, solution, hunches, insights for applicability.

Obstacles which inhibit creativity

1 **Negativity in individuals and in teams:** focusing on the negative aspects of a problem as opposed to using your energy to seek opportunities for a solution.
2 **Fear of failure:** a fear of appearing foolish in front of colleagues.
3 **Lack of quality thinking time and experiences to draw from:** being over-stressed can make it difficult to think objectively and inhibits the natural thinking process.

4   **Over-conformance with rules and regulations, a
    lack of freedom to develop:** too many rules can
    encourage mental laziness.
5   **Making assumptions that are not necessarily true:**
    failing to identify the assumptions you are making will
    inhibit the process of developing new ideas.
6   **Applying too much logic and not listening to the
    depth mind:** too much logic excludes imagination,
    intuition and synthesis from your thought process.
7   **Thinking you are not creative:** the biggest barrier of
    all!

The non-creative person

These obstacles can be seen in the profile of the non-creative
person; someone who is:

- not able to think positively about problems (and does
  not see them as opportunities)
- too busy or stressed to think objectively or at all
- very self-critical
- timid in putting forward a new idea (fearing ridicule)
- viewed as a conformist by friends/colleagues
- prone to apply logic as a first and last resort
- sceptical that many people are capable of being
  creative
- unable to think laterally
- uninspired even when confronted with a new idea.

On the other hand, creativity can be encouraged in people (including oneself) by exploring some of the qualities and characteristics of creative thinkers and the activities and steps that can be undertaken to improve the processes involved.

Developing creativity

To be creative an individual should:

1 **Think beyond the invisible frameworks that surround problems and situations.**
  Think 'outside of the box'. Be open to new observations and thoughts, however ridiculous they may seem at first. We tend to see what we expect to be there but if we opened our minds beyond the 'normal' we would be more observant, objective and creative in our thoughts. Considering a new starting point and perspective when looking for a solution can be very inspiring. Approaching the problem from a different angle can encourage new ideas. Creative thinking should be an adventure into the unknown.

2 **Recognise when assumptions are being made and challenge them.**
  Never assume anything as you are making the supposition that it is correct or true. Preconceptions are the ideas you have before you gain actual knowledge. Assumptions and preconceptions are often unwarranted and misleading, and are great blockers to creative thinking. Challenging assumptions can open up a whole new creative process.

3 **Spot blinkered thinking and widen the field of vision (to draw on the experiences of other individuals and businesses).**

It is very easy to only 'think within the box' when you are faced with a problem but if you widen your parameters the answers may be closer than you think. Technologies and practices in industries other than your own may spark an idea, leading to a solution. Travel can widen your horizons and your span of relevance and open up all sorts of new avenues for thought.

4 **Develop and adapt ideas from more than one source.**

As humans we cannot make something out of nothing, our minds need something to work on, so we combine ideas and elements which are already in existence, to create new ideas and products. The creative mind can see possibilities, bonds and connections between various elements which others cannot see.

5 **Practice serendipity (finding valuable and agreeable things when not particularly seeking them) – having a wide attention span and range of interests is important.**

When we're involved in trying to solve a problem we tend to have a narrow focus but we should always be open and aware of the unexpected. What may seem irrelevant at first could later become significant in creative thinking. It may take a while, perhaps weeks, months or even years, which is why the creative thinker should retain as much information and as many experiences as possible.

It's these experiences that may be the trigger to a creative thought which might just solve a difficult problem.

6 'Transfer technology' from one field to another.
Keep an open mind when faced with a problem and look outside of your own situation. Often other departments, organisations and industries can give you the inspiration to develop ideas to solve your challenges. The most successful creative thinkers have knowledge about more than one field and often make their names appear in quite a different sphere than they are normally associated with.

7 Be open and prepared to use chance or unpredictable things and events to your advantage.
Have a wide focus of attention and develop your powers of observation to make use of the chance happenings you come across in your life. Use your experience to interpret these things as something useful without having preconceptions. You may have to invest a lot of time exposing yourself to chance experiences but they will give you a good reference base for future creativity.

8 Explore thought processes and the key elements of the mind at work in analysing, valuing and synthesising.
Creative thinking cannot really be broken down into a specific process or system. The very nature of creativity can mean it is a disorderly process. However, we usually begin by analysing the problem in hand and then playing around with restructuring it (synthesising). Next we set about using our imaginations and valuing the thoughts

we have in relation to a possible solution. We should be aware of these thought processes and use them to our advantage, not let them get in the way of being creative.

9 **Use his/her 'depth' mind (the unconscious mind) for example by sleeping on a problem to generate creative solutions and ideas.**

The value of 'sleeping on a problem' has been long known. Apart from actually dreaming of a solution, the time in bed before you sleep is very relaxing and allows ideas to be generated. Dreams allow you mind a total freedom to make connections you would not normally consider. Although this may not give you the exact answer it could be enough to direct your waking thoughts in the right direction. You should note down your dream thoughts as soon as you wake so they are not lost.

The brain is capable of analysing information that you may not even realise you have absorbed. By switching off your conscious thinking you allow your depth mind to begin analysing, valuing and synthesising your inner most knowledge. You cannot control this type of inspiration but you should stay alert and expectant, so you are aware when it shows itself.

10 **Note down thoughts/ideas that apparently drop into the mind unsolicited so that they are not forgotten.**

Keeping a notebook is a good way of recording materials for your future use. Make notes of conversations (real or from TV or radio), quotations from articles or books and observations and thoughts. Your instinct will tell you what may be relevant to future problem solving and creative thinking. There is no need to be too systematic as when you look back through your notes you will make connections between points which you didn't initially see.

11 Use analogy (to improve imaginative thinking) to find 'models' or solutions in 'nature', in existing products, services and/or in other organisations – not always reinventing the wheel.
Nature holds many answers to our problems. We have the challenge of realising them and applying what we discover to our individual situation. Other models can be found in existing products and organisations but we must be aware not to copy them directly as this could lead to more problems. We should keep an open mind and be very observant when looking at our surroundings and use what we see to our advantage.

12 Try to sometimes make the strange familiar and the familiar strange to spark new ideas.
Creative thinking is the search for something new. Sometimes that something new can be found within the familiar. By making the familiar strange you begin to look at it differently and this can lead to many creative thoughts. The reverse is also true. By becoming more familiar with the strange you open your mind to exploring new avenues you may not have realised existed. Both these processes can lead the creative thinker to new ideas.

13 **Make connections with points that are apparently irrelevant, disguised/buried or not easily accessible, outside your own sphere of expertise and lacking authority.**

Look beyond the 'normal' for your inspiration. Learn to think freely about a situation or problem and don't be too hasty about defining a problem and boxing it into a category. Look outside of your knowledge sphere for the answers.

14 **Suspend judgement to encourage the creative process and avoid premature criticism – analysis and criticism repress creativity.**

Criticism has it's place but shouldn't be embarked upon too early in the creative process as it can have a negative effect. When exploring and experimenting with new ideas, too much negativity can cut short the creative flow. Constructive criticism should be invited when you reach the evaluating and testing stage.

15 **Know when to leave a problem (remaining aware but detached) for solutions to emerge – patience is important here as is the suspension of judgement.**

Sometimes you can be too involved with a problem and you need to take a step back to be able to make progress. By switching off your attention you allow your depth mind to become more active. You need to have the confidence that your unconscious mind will take over. Ideas often appear when you are involved in another activity, such as driving, sitting on a train or walking. Try to resist the temptation to start thinking consciously about the ideas that come to you in this way, and instead allow them to develop in their own time.

16 Tolerate ambiguity and occasionally live with doubt and uncertainty.

Successful creative thinkers are able to tolerate ambiguity, uncertainty, complexity and apparent disorder in their quest for a solution. It can be difficult to resist coming to a premature conclusion or solution. The challenge is to hold many ideas in your mind at once and to work with them to a satisfactory conclusion.

17 Stimulate your own curiosity (in everything including travel) and the skills of observation, listening, reading and recording.

Curiosity is the appetite of the intellect. Creative thinkers are naturally curious because they have a desire to learn, know and develop new ideas. Curiosity in creative thinking is a great motivator; it's the thought of 'I wonder what will happen next?' That is the link between thinking and learning.

Travel can be a great mental stimulant, arousing a curiosity and interest in the world and other cultures. Experiencing other cultures can make you 'wake up' to the one you normally live in and put a different perspective on it.

Reading requires your mind to be imaginative and creative. Always stay alert when reading as books, newspapers and other matter are all sources of ideas, thoughts, facts and opinions, which, taken out of context may be relevant to your present or future thinking.

Good listening skills rely on a certain amount of humility – the understanding that we don't know everything. Having an open mind and being curious when you are listening, allows you to really absorb what you are hearing without being critical and analytical. Make sure you fully understand what you are hearing before you analyse and evaluate. Don't easily dismiss what may seem like useless information but be curious enough to see if you can develop it into something more.

Remember

Managers should remember that creativity should challenge the status quo to test continuously for improvements, because:

- a thing is not right because we do it
- a method is not good because we use it
- equipment is not the best because we own it.

Decision-making and the creative thinker

Decision-making is an attribute which is mastered by all successful creative thinkers. Many effective decisions have to be made throughout the creative process.

The effective thinker and decision maker is skilled in analysing, synthesising and valuing. He knows when and how to use his depth mind and he's tuned in to his intuitive mind. His imagination can help to find new ways of approaching situations and problems. He is always open to new ideas, even if they come via unlikely analogies as his span of relevance is wide. He has enough self awareness to know that others may have a greater specialised knowledge than he, and he is able to consult with them in the search for solutions and the truth.

To make an effective decision these six processes should be followed:

1 Define the objective
2 Gather sufficient information
3 Identify the options
4 Evaluate those options
5 Make the decision, choose the option to follow
6 Test its implementation.

The three essential skills of an effective decision-maker and creative thinker are:

1 analysing
2 synthesising
3 valuing.

Effective decisions result from thinking things through using the crucial elements of:

- establishing the facts
- considering all the options
- deciding on the course of action.

The truly effective creative thinker:

- has skills of analysis, synthesis and valuing
- is open to intuition
- has imagination
- is open to new ideas

- has a sense of humility – recognising that others may have better powers or knowledge and combining these with their own ideas.

Never make false assumptions or jump to conclusions. Don't be prone to faulty reasoning or to not listening to others. Always operate in the context of facing reality and of seeking and speaking the truth.

The logical or rational creative thinker will follow this decision-making model:

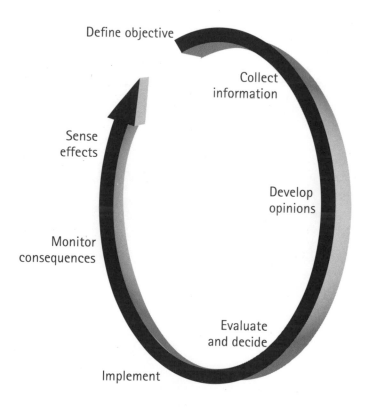

Define objective

Collect information

Sense effects

Develop opinions

Monitor consequences

Evaluate and decide

Implement

Decision makers don't always choose the optimum solution as they are affected by emotion, power, politics, the influences of other people and by their own values. Often a decision is a compromise between different courses of action, being one that:

- agrees to some extent with one's own personal interests, needs or values
- meets the value standards of superiors
- is acceptable to those affected (by the decision and for carrying it out)
- looks reasonable
- has an escape element of self-justification if it all goes wrong.

Clearly such approaches to decision-making must be removed from your approach!

Managers need to be prepared to make time to think creatively about decisions – to devote quality time to this crucial area of activity, because the **thought behind the solution is as important as the action itself**.

Key elements of creative thinking and decision-making

Analysis

The ability to break up the whole into more manageable parts, dissecting complex matters into simple elements.

An analytical mind can:
* establish the relationship between the parts and the whole
* find the root cause(s) of the problem
* identify the issue(s) at stake.

Analytical, logical thinking is the ability of being able to draw proper conclusions from the information available.

Analytical ability together with the knowledge of how to develop and use analytical techniques is not enough for real achievement as a creative thinker. You also need flair, perseverance and self-motivation to be really successful. Analysis plays an important role in problem solving. It helps to sift through facts and opinions, dissecting the problem into parts and moving you towards a solution to the problem. The hallmarks of an analytical mind are:
* simplicity,
* originality; and
* clarity.

Analytical ability can be improved by:
* working from first principles
* establishing the facts and separating them from opinions, assumptions or suppositions

- asking questions such as 'When did the problem first arise?' and considering Who, What, When, Why, Where and How
- constantly checking the logical steps which can undermine good reasoning
- thinking backwards from the desired outcome
- organising the facts
- seeing the problem as a solution in disguise.

Two other terms with regard to logical thinking are 'inductive' and 'deductive'. These are both ways of inferring things: deduction is a means of drawing a particular inference from a general proposition, while induction is the forming of a generalisation from a number of particular instances.

To test your logical thinking ability, consider the following two scenarios:

1 A businessman on the way to a meeting has some time to kill. He is in a small town and decides to have his hair cut. The town has only two barbers, each with his own shop. The businessman looked through the window of one shop and saw that it was extremely untidy. The barber needed a shave, his clothes were unkempt and his hair was badly cut. The other shop was extremely tidy. The barber was freshly shaved, impeccably dressed and his hair was neatly trimmed. The businessman returned to the first shop for his haircut. Why?

2 Two trains are 100 miles apart. They are moving towards each other, one at 40mph and the other at 60mph. A plane flying backwards and forwards

between the two trains is travelling at 80mph. How far does the plane fly before the trains meet?

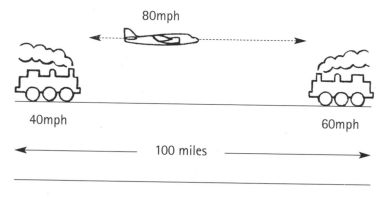

80mph

40mph

60mph

100 miles

Don't spend more than 10 minutes on each scenario then turn to the Appendix on page 97 for the answers.

Often the end result is clear, the problem is how to get there. Using your imagination to visualise the end result, work backwards logically to find out the solution. Using this method try to solve the following problem.

3   Sandra has to get her two babies, Jennifer and Carl, as well as her cat, out to the car. Because Sandra has a broken arm she can only carry one baby or the cat at a time. Neither child can be left alone with the cat. How does she get all three of them to the car in as few trips as possible?

The solution to this problem is in the Appendix on page 97.

Part of the process of logical thinking is re-arranging the available information. A problem is often a jumble of information that needs to be:

- Separated into its component parts
- Re-arranged or restructured

A problem is often a solution in disguise. Try sorting out the available information in a systematic way. Sometimes using a pen and paper as a tool is a great strategy. Consider the following scenario:

4   Louise, Donna and Jane live next door to each other. Donna has the flat in the middle. They work as a teacher, a TV presenter and a nurse, but not necessarily in that order. The TV presenter walks Jane's dog when Jane is working late. The teacher taps on Louise's wall when Louise's music is too loud. What career does each woman have?

The solution to this problem is in the Appendix on page 97.

Logical thinking is only a small part of effective creative thinking. It can be very useful but be conscious not to over-analyse as it can lead to inactivity or 'paralysis by analysis'.

Synthesis

Synthesis is the opposite to analysis, it is the ability to combine parts or elements to form a whole. 'Holistic' is a useful word to explain this approach. 'Wholes' are produced by grouping units together where it is difficult to analyse them into their parts without losing the wholeness. When thinking creatively, there is a need to be able to see the wood for the trees (holism) rather then just the trees (analysis).

The ability to be able to think about organisations and teams, opportunities and problems as wholes is extremely important. In business, the whole is greater than the sum of the parts. Creative thinkers in business need to see the whole view to be able to yield solutions. It is not productive to see things just as a marketing problem or a production problem, for example. By deliberately refraining from analytical thinking beyond a certain point, synthesis will take over and the whole will take shape.

The Gestalt school of psychology bases itself on the following principles:
- the overall significance of behaviour rather than a mechanistic explanation
- the relationship between events, rather than just the events themselves
- events don't happen in isolation, but in a context which gives them significance.

Managers without holistic minds tend to take a narrow view of problems, seeing them related only to a single function, e.g. 'This is a Marketing problem'.

When we synthesise we are putting elements together to make a compound. This is how ideas can begin as seeds and grow inside our minds.

The idea of ideas growing can bring a reluctance to analyse ideas too early, but rather to let them develop before submitting them for criticism from others. By becoming more aware of holistic thinking and it's importance you will be able to deliberately refrain from analysis and develop the skills to allow the whole to take shape in your mind.

Valuing

Valuing is the third essential skill in effective thinking and decision-making. To make decisions you must be able:

- to establish the true facts; and
- to know what to do.

Time should be taken to discover the true facts as this will make knowing what to do easier. In the process of establishing the truth we use the skill of valuing alongside analysis, synthesis, depth mind and intuition.

Another form of valuing is knowing who to trust and when to trust to get the truth. This is where educated intuition comes in. Questioning is a valid method of establishing the credentials of the adviser and the credibility of the advice. Experience will help you to recognise the people who:

- tell you what they think you want to hear
- express a view thinking it will agree with your own
- are watching their backs
- try to hide things.

Be scrupulous in establishing the truth as bad advisers may give you interpretations of the situation which are from their objective. They may give you information to help you follow a particular course of action which they want you to follow. Beware of inaccurate figures, errors in facts and assumptions as they will divert you from the truth. You should try to surround yourself with advisers you can trust, who are in touch with the reality around them and who are loyal to their commitment to truth. By the same means, be willing to admit when you are wrong, you will be setting a good example.

Other useful approaches to creative thinking and decision-making

Imaginative thinking

Being imaginative is part of being creative in the approach to decision-making. It is a form of holistic thinking which can be used to originate and innovate to find solutions. We can use it to surprise the competition, to exploit the unexpected, to invent new products or services, or to solve problems creatively.

An imaginative person can:
- recall events easily and visually
- foresee what may happen before an event actually takes place
- be creative artistically, mechanically or verbally.

All these elements contribute to the process of creative thinking.

There are a range of imaginative abilities which can be used by the creative thinker:
- **Recalling:** to be able to bring something back into the mind that is not actually present at that time.
- **Visualising:** to be able to form a picture in the mind of something not experienced, such as a walk on a faraway beach or the moon.
- **Creating:** to be able to form an image of something that doesn't exist at present.

- **Foreseeing:** to be able to see a development or an outcome before it actually happens or takes place.
- **Fantasy:** to be able to invent the unreal by changing or combining elements of reality with no logical constraints.

A good manager, trying to work out a problem, needs to be both imaginative and careful about the facts they use to ensure they properly deduce the solution. They must think imaginatively but be coherent, methodical and in touch with the reality of the situation at hand.

Imagination should not be your number one skill in creative thinking but it should feature as part of your skill set.

Being imaginative can lead us to be innovative, inventive, exploring, risk-taking and adventuring. It is an aid to creative thinking but we must remember to stay in touch with the true facts of the situation or problem in hand.

John Sainsbury, chairman of the highly successful chain of supermarkets, states:

> ❝ The characteristic in a good manager which I appreciate almost above all else is that of imagination. The good manager has to be imaginative in order to be a successful innovator. Success in that respect brings not only a valuable contribution to any enterprise, but also the considerable personal satisfaction of creative achievement.
>
> It is imagination which is needed to anticipate events and to respond to change. It is only those with a lively imagination who can really develop a sensitive understanding of others, be they customers, colleagues or shop floor workers. To be able to do that is a vital ingredient of success in commerce and industry. ❞

Practice using your imagination by imagining yourself in five years time as the chief executive of your organisation. Create a credible scenario to explain your rise to this position. Use all your senses to really flesh out the fantasy.

Conceptual thinking

In many cases the analyst is trying to break down the particulars of a problem or situation into something more general and less concrete. This is known as 'abstracting' but this term can generate unpleasant overtones in some people, such as:

- It's difficult to understand
- It's remote from apprehension
- It's insufficiently factual
- It's theoretical
- It's impersonal
- It's detached
- It's visionary.

To think conceptually is a similar process to analysis but a concept should be thought about holistically. A concept is something conceived in the mind. It can come from the practice of analysis but it is different in that it is a whole and is an entity that can be developed in its own right.

Conceptual thinking in business addresses such issues as:

- What business are we in?
- What are its strengths and weaknesses?
- What are its purposes and aims?

Concepts grow with the aid of creative thinking, reading, listening, experience and our depth mind. The quality of your concepts and your ability to develop them through creative thinking is a basis for good decision-making.

Intuition

Intuition can be described as an instinct, a first impression, a feel, a hunch, a sense or flair.

Being intuitive is undoubtedly a help in creative thinking and decision-making. It can be said to be a form of valuing done without conscious effort and carried out very quickly. The intuitive person discerns the truth about a situation or a person almost instantly.

Intuition is central to the way successful thinkers work. It is an unconscious ability to select the right option or evaluation, a recognition of truth from the depth mind.

To be more aware and in touch with your intuition even if it is only a faint whisper. To recognise it you need to trust your intuitive powers. You should be prepared to give your intuition the benefit of the doubt but also be aware it can be affected by your emotions surrounding the situation or problem. Stress and tiredness can upset the intuitive thinkers immediate comprehension of the reality of a situation so remember to evaluate your intuitive thoughts carefully.

CHECKLIST: HOW DOES YOUR MIND WORK?

- Consider how developed your mind is at using: Analysis, Synthesis and Valuing. Which is the most developed and which the least?

  _____

  _____

- Can you recall an experience of using your depth mind to synthesise two or more different courses of action?

  _____

  _____

continued

- Can you recall putting an issue to one side and then finding your mind has discovered a solution while you weren't consciously looking for one?

  _____

  _____

- Would you consider yourself an analyst or more of a holistic thinker?

  _____

  _____

- How much do you rely on your intuition when meeting new people?

  _____

  _____

- Can you recall being aware that your depth mind has evaluated something after the event when you weren't conscious of it?

  _____

  _____

- Do you balance spending time thinking with spending time interacting with others?

  _____

  _____

- Can you recall visually things that you have experienced with great accuracy?

  _____

  _____

continued

- Can you visualise things that you have not experienced?

  _____

  _____

- Do you find it easy to use your imagination to choose colour schemes to decorate a room, or think up stories to tell your children?

  _____

  _____

- Do you use all of your five senses when imagining situations?

  _____

  _____

Using creative thinking to evaluate the options

You should choose a course of action out of a range of 'options'. You should never assume that there is only one option open to you. Consider a number of options, as many as you can think of. Information gathering will help you to collect options. Even consider options that you think might be closed to you; for example, price increases.

'Possible' options are those which include everything that could be done within the limits of the situation. Whereas 'feasible' options are those that can be put in place using the existing resources.

The first step in evaluating options is to sort out the feasible options from the possible options. Then, working only with the feasible options reduce them to two alternatives – the either/or. The process of evaluation then allows you to opt for one of them, both of them, or you could consider combining, mixing or blending them.

This process resembles a funnel:

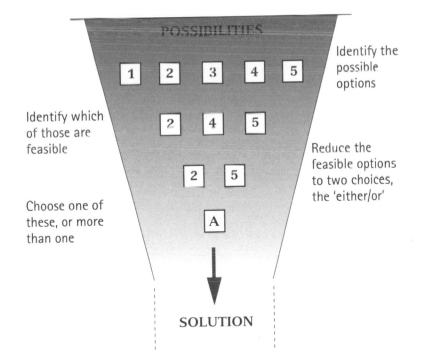

POSSIBILITIES

1 2 3 4 5   Identify the possible options

Identify which of those are feasible

2 4 5

Reduce the feasible options to two choices, the 'either/or'

2 5

Choose one of these, or more than one

A

SOLUTION

You may also need to consider whether any action is necessary at all, either now or later. The final strategy would be to consider keeping your options open and not making the final choice just yet.

CHECKLIST: OPTIONS

Throughout the creative decision-making process consider the following and make notes:

- Which options are feasible?

  _____

  _____

- Which of the feasible options are practical alternatives?

  _____

  _____

- Are they mutually exclusive, or can we use both, or a combination of the two?

  _____

  _____

- Will the result they bring achieve the objective we set out to meet?

  _____

  _____

continued

Whilst considering the options be aware of making sure you have all the correct facts. Factors which can limit the range and choice of options include:

- **Time:** How much have we got? Is it enough? Is someone else dictating the time limit? Can it be altered and with what consequences?
- **Information:** Do we have all the relevant data? Do we have enough to make an informed judgement? Is the information we have reliable?
- **Resources:** Do we have enough funding? Do we have the correct machinery and the staff to operate it?
- **Knowledge:** Do we know enough about the field we are in or are entering? Are our managers and staff fully trained and up to speed?

Generating options through creative thinking and innovation will usually lead to better decision-making. Judgement should be suspended while generating options to allow the free flow of creativity. The ability to consider fresh possibilities can increase the range of options. Do not be too eager to settle for the 'good option' too early, there may be a much better one just around the corner.

Be aware of the negative critic who may not be open minded enough to consider all the options and may distract you from making the right judgements. You can recognise them as they use phases such as:

- It won't work
- We always do it this way
- It can't be done
- It failed before
- It costs too much
- I don't like that idea
- It's impractical.

Calculating the risks

In weighing up the options you must consider the possible and the probable consequences. Judgement and experience should be used to select from the range of options which have been carefully assessed in light of all the facts. The desired outcome will be one that realises the purpose, aims and objectives of the organisation.

It is quite often the case in business that the larger the risk the greater the potential gain. But risks should be carefully calculated and as much done as possible to minimise them. This is an assessment of the risk and reward. Can you accept the risk of failure? If the risks are too great the strength of mind needs to be found to say 'no' before the idea is implemented and the consequences become reality.

Key questions to ask yourself to avoid making a bad decision:

- Have I defined the objective correctly?
- Do I have sufficient information?
- Have I considered all the feasible options?
- Have a evaluated all the options correctly?
- Does the decision 'feel right' now I've begun to implement it?

If you do make a mistake, identify where you made it. This will help commit the information to your depth mind and enable you to learn from experience.

Innovation

Team innovation

Communicating about innovation

Brainstorming

Two more methods of collecting ideas

Dealing with change and overcoming
obstacles to innovation

Criticism

Part two: Innovation

The process of innovation

The innovative process has three main stages:

1 **Generation of ideas:** individuals and teams producing new ideas and improving existing ones.
2 **Harvesting ideas:** the act of gathering the ideas, sifting through them and evaluating them.
3 **Developing and implementing the ideas:** the research, testing, improvement and development of the ideas and their implementation.

To innovate is to introduce something new – an idea, method or device – it is a combination of two processes: generating new ideas and the implementation of them. Innovation is a type of change which can be either a series of steps or one huge leap towards in a desired direction.

Innovation calls for good leadership and management at all levels of the organisation. Good leaders will stimulate people to be more 'hands on' and interested in their work, and in turn, this will lead to the generation of more good ideas. Managerial leaders are needed for change to be able to happen and change brings about the need for leaders.

A general interest in all things leads to ideas. The recognition by management of these ideas leads to greater job interest, a deeper involvement and commitment from staff. But innovation is more than having new ideas; it is about successfully implementing them – turning ideas into useful, practical and commercial products or services. Most change happens gradually, a development of existing ideas, products and services.

Everyone can participate in team creativity and innovation. Everyone is capable of using creativity, experience and ingenuity to implement change.

Some of the key players in an organisation who are responsible for innovation:

Creative thinker: produces new and original ideas

Innovator: brings new products/services to the market or changes existing ones

Inventor: produces new and commercial ideas

Entrepreneur: conceives or receives ideas and translates them into business reality to exploit a market opportunity

Intrapreneur: responsible for innovation within an organisation

Champion: has the determination and commitment to implement an idea

Sponsor: backs an idea and helps remove obstacles

Effective innovation requires:

1 a blend of new ideas
2 the ability to get things done
3 sound commercial sense
4 customer focus
5 a conducive organisational climate.

Five factors to create the right climate for innovation

1 **Management commitment**

   Top management needs to visibly show their recognition and commitment to innovation; to encourage and facilitate a good attitude to change at all levels. Without a leadership team that values new ideas and who constantly struggles to keep moving towards innovation, there will be no sustained and profitable growth.

2 **Positive strategic change**

   Organisations should consider the following questions:
   - What is our business?
   - Where is our business at this time?
   - What do we want to achieve in three to five years' time?
   - What do we want to achieve in ten years' time?
   - What are our strengths and weaknesses?
   - Have we got the necessary resources to enable us to implement our strategic plans?
   - What are our competitors' plans? Do they pose a threat to our plans?
   - Are we equipped to deal with the unforeseen?

3 **A long-term perspective**

   Innovation should not be reactive but be part of a long-term strategic plan under the direction of good leaders and managers.

4   **Flexibility to deal with change**
    Flexibility is a key quality in dealing with change
    in an organisation. This can mean flattening the
    hierarchical management pyramid and pushing
    decision-making downwards. Effective, open
    communication at all staff levels is essential for
    this to happen.

5   **Accepting the possibility of risk**
    New ideas nearly always come with an element of risk
    but the possibility of failure shouldn't be used as an
    excuse not to innovate. Managers should be aware of
    risks and face the possibility of terminating potential
    failures before too much damage is done. However,
    management should not be too critical if mistakes
    occur as this will smother initiative in the long-term.

Innovation and organisation

Organisations need a certain amount of order in them; rules
and procedures to be followed, but individuals also need a
certain amount of freedom – without it they're innovative
thoughts are curtailed. Freedom of thought leads to people
expressing themselves and being creative and innovative.

Management structures that are as flat as possible are more
conducive to informal and flexible relationships in an
organisation. These types of structures permit and encourage
different departments to communicate and cross-fertilise.

Managers tend to be people who like order but they need to be aware that innovation is often a disorderly process. Although control is an important leadership function it should be exercised with skill and sensitivity. Organisations need to find a balance between structure and productivity, and innovation and creativity. An organisation which is only interested in reproducing existing products and services would soon go out of existence as technological and market advances are made all around them.

Characteristics of an innovative organisation

- The management is personal and informal
- There is not a strong emphasis on functional speciali-sation
- Workers have been allowed to have freedom of thought
- The management structure is quite flat with leaders being very approachable
- Clearly laid down procedures are kept to a minimum
- Workers are encouraged to be creative and flexible, and to develop themselves.

A bureaucratic organisation is the opposite of this. Over the years, and as companies grow in size, they increase their bureaucratic tendency. Paper proliferates and even minor decisions start to be referred upwards. Systems regulate people and become restrictive. Senior managers become more remote and people gradually feel isolated and alienated. This curbs innovation and creativity.

To be successful at innovation organisations should apply five main ingredients to their management style:

1 Top level commitment

This must be visible and audible and top management must ensure that blocks are removed and that inhibiting bureaucracy/individuals does not foul up the process. Chief executives and senior managers must value new ideas and innovation, and participate actively to ensure that all know of their commitment to positive and useful change. Sometimes the need for short-term profits can dull the edge of creativity and innovation. Only top management can prevent this happening – taking the long not the short-term view.

2 Flexible in organisational structure

The antithesis of the innovative organisation is the bureaucratic one and Weber's characteristics of bureaucratic organisations are as follows:
- authority is impersonal and formal
- strong emphasis on functional specialisation
- a rule for every eventuality
- strong emphasis on hierarchy and status
- clearly laid down procedures (red tape)
- proliferation of paperwork
- security of employment and advancement by seniority.

At the opposite end of the scale would be the flexible organisation which is one:
- capable of responding to changing situations
- where barriers between staff in different areas are minimised

- with a flat rather than pyramid organisational structure
- where decision-making is pushed downwards to where the organisation meets its customers/suppliers
- with entrepreneurial flair present at all levels
- which can develop and test more than one solution to problems encountered
- with efficient rather than stifling monitoring systems
- which has enough 'discipline' to get things done
- which balances freedom and order.

3   **Tolerant of failure**
    Innovation and risk go hand in hand. Management which goes into critical overdrive when mistakes occur (rather than analysing them to learn from the failures) smothers creativity and innovation. Risks can yield failure, but not taking risks can spell total disaster and an end to profits and growth. Unless failure results from negligence, recklessness or complete incompetence, managers should not seek out scapegoats or exact revenge. Profits are the reward for taking risks and innovative organisations learn to live with risk.

4   **Encouraging teamwork and innovation**
    In innovation it can be said that none of us is as good as all of us. Teamwork and innovation are better in organisations where:
    - the climate is open
    - participation is encouraged
    - facts and information are readily available

- change is managed positively
- resources are provided for training and development
- rules are at a minimum (with policies and guidelines instead)
- internal communications are good and more by mouth than memo
- respect is given to all colleagues (but not on demand by management – it has to be earned)
- managers are themselves highly motivated
- teamwork often transcends departmental boundaries.

5 **Good at open and constructive communication**

Communication should be good laterally **and** vertically (and flatter organisations should – in theory, at least – encourage good lateral communication). Managers should ensure a good flow of information – ideas can emerge as a result. Cross-fertilisation can create more (and better) ideas, particularly where departmental, divisional boundaries are crossed. Feedback about ideas can maintain interest levels and information about progress can stimulate further activity. Good communication can improve innovation and should:

- stress the importance of new ideas and show how the business has improved because of their implementation
- indicate why ideas have been rejected or accepted
- give progress reports of ideas originated by individuals and teams
- recognise and reward appropriately for successful innovation.

CHECKLIST FOR THE INNOVATIVE ORGANISATION

- Is the top management team committed to innovation?

  _____

- Does the organisation express clearly its vision (which should include an emphasis on innovation)?

  _____

- Is the Chief Executive openly enthusiastic for change?

  _____

- Are mutual stimulation, feedback and constructive criticism all at high levels of activity?

  _____

- Is the organisation good at team work including the use of project teams?

  _____

- Are mistakes and failures accepted as part of risk-taking?

  _____

- Do creative people join _and_ stay with the organisation?

  _____

continued

CHECKLIST FOR THE INNOVATIVE ORGANISATION continued

- Is innovation rewarded (financially or by promotion or both)?

  _____

- Are lateral communications good?

  _____

- Can ideas be exchanged informally and are opportunities provided to do this?

  _____

- Does the organisation raise excuses not to innovate?

  _____

- Are resources given to new ideas?

  _____

- Is the structure flexible?

  _____

- Is decision-making pushed down to the lowest level at which decisions could be taken?

  _____

- Do all staff see themselves as part of the creative and innovative processes?

  _____

continued

CHECKLIST FOR THE INNOVATIVE ORGANISATION continued

- Does the organisation take a long-term view of the benefits of innovation?

  _____

- Is innovation part of the organisation's vision and strategy?

  _____

- Is it fun to work in your organisation?

  _____

What qualities should a chief executive as a leader have?

A chief executive should have the ability to build teamwork and build a team approach at every level of an organisation. They should be able to make the most arduous work interesting and create a good team spirit amongst workers.

The chief executive should have the ability to:
- think deeply
- communicate clearly and openly
- implement and manage change
- project infectious enthusiasm and have a sense of humour.

A successful chief executive will have a team of executives and administrators who can think strategically and build the corporate culture towards greater teamwork. They will have the knowledge and ability to get results from the individuals who make up the workforce. This is known as action-centred leadership and is a means of realising a company's potential. This is a recognition of the need to lead rather than merely manage. Some of the best organisations are led by a team rather than an individual but the team itself needs a leader. This is the core responsibility of the chief executive.

Sir Raymond Lygo, former head of British Aerospace and a former admiral in the Royal Navy, says:

> "Management is the art of organisation, the art of organising people and things to produce and achieve objectives. Leadership is the ability to inspire other men and women to achieve things much greater than they would have done if they were left to their own devices."

All organisations that aspire to innovate need both leadership and management to achieve productive order without sacrificing freedom and creativity. Chief executives should give their organisations a sense of direction and a clear vision of the future. They should also be able to guide their organisations towards that clear vision.

Motivation and innovation

Innovation will not happen without motivation. People must want to innovate, they need to be enthusiastic and interested in the subject at hand. It is important to recruit people who have the potential for this. This type of person tends to be adventurous and independently-minded. Young people are often more future-orientated and open to new experiences, with fewer preconceptions and assumptions. Therefore, it is good for organisations to recruit intelligent, enthusiastic and creative young people who have a willingness to put new ideas into practice.

Characteristics to look for when recruiting

- A superior general intelligence with an ability to store and recall information
- A high degree of autonomy, self-sufficiency and self-direction
- Relatively little gregariousness; creative thinkers tend to be ambivert
- An independence of judgement and a resilience to group pressure towards conformity in thinking
- A sense of honesty and the ability to express that honesty
- A broad range of interests to stimulate the mind
- A special motivation to solve problems and to take up the opportunities to do this
- A sense of curiosity and good powers of observation
- Dedication and commitment to projects

- An awareness of the purposeful unconscious mind
- An ability to hold many ideas together in creative tension, without reaching a premature resolution.

But, remember, selection is a two way process. Creative people are looking for an environment which allows them to explore their talents and for those talents to flourish. Otherwise they become stifled and frustrated.

What do innovative people expect from the organisation they work for?

1 **Recognition and appreciation:** There is often a delay between an innovative idea and the results of that creative work. To encourage the continuation of that creativity it is important for management to show appreciation and to give recognition as soon as possible, even if the idea has to go through much more development before it comes to fruition.

2 **The freedom to work outside normal department boundaries in areas of particular interest:** Creative people are most effective if they are allowed to work in the areas which interest them the greatest.

3 **Contact with colleagues outside of there normal team:** Conversation, both formal and informal, with colleagues from different departments can be very stimulating for the creative person. Random meetings in communal areas often generate new thoughts and ideas.

4   **Encouragement to take risks:** Innovations all have a
    certain amount of risk attached to them. Management
    should encourage calculated risks while being aware
    of potential disasters.

These environmental conditions are motivational to the
creative person and give them the drive they need to move
forward. Without these conditions creative and innovative
flair can't flourish. This will lead to a team of unhappy
workers with very low motivation.

Distinctive characteristics of the creative leader

- **A willingness to accept risk:** By giving workers a
  freedom to be creative you take on a certain amount
  of risk of failures or financial losses. As a leader you
  should not abdicate risk but take some responsibility
  for it. You should be aware and sensitive to possible
  consequences from an innovative idea. Do not dwell
  on mistakes – learn from them and use that knowledge
  to make better decisions about future innovations.
- **An ability to develop half-formed ideas:** New ideas
  are rarely fully formed, they can take much development. Do not easily dismiss an ill-formed idea as it
  may be the basis of a great one. Leaders should listen
  and facilitate team creativity to develop ideas further.
- **An ability to be flexible:** Rules and systems have
  their place but they shouldn't be restrictive to creative
  people. Sometimes procedures should be stretched if

they can't be broken. Don't get bogged down in organisational treacle.

- **An ability to respond quickly:** Some new ideas need to be actioned quickly. Leaders should be able to deploy resources without having to delay by referring to top management.
- **A personal enthusiasm:** Highly motivated leaders impart that enthusiasm onto their workers. This leads to intellectual stimulation and the generation of ideas.

Creative leadership is the kind of leadership that encourages, stimulates and guides the process of innovation from beginning to end. The challenge is in leading creative people to reach their full potential.

With these characteristics managers should be able to:
- Manage for creativity and innovation
- Provide an organisational environment in which innovation can thrive
- Use a variety of techniques to stimulate ideas for products, services and systems, and to generate ideas for bringing these to fruition.

To manage innovation and to draw 'greatness' out of people, the following process is used to guide individuals and teams:
1 **Defining the task:** clearly explains what needs to be accomplished or what area needs to be considered.
2 **Planning:** the organisation of resources – people, materials and time.
3 **Briefing:** makes sure all participants know their role and importance.
4 **Controlling:** keeps people on track without being too restrictive.

5   **Evaluating:** makes insightful judgements and appropriate criticism as necessary.
6   **Motivating:** keeps interest in and commitment to the task.
7   **Organising:** keeps structure within the project team.
8   **Setting an example:** practices the behaviours needed to be seen in others.
9   **Supporting:** builds and maintains a team spirit and is accessible at all times.

The generation of ideas

It is interesting to note that organisations can get ideas from, amongst other sources:

- R&D (internal or external)
- Staff
- Competitors
- Suppliers
- Customers
- Quality circles.

One survey demonstrated that SMEs (small and medium-sized enterprises) can get ideas from, in order of importance:

1   Staff
2   Customers
3   Market and competition
4   Board and Planning Group
5   Sales department
6   Suppliers
7   Managing director

8   Consultants

9   Shows and exhibitions.

Ideas have to be sieved – by individuals or by teams – to choose and refine the selected ideas to be developed. When selecting ideas the following criteria should be considered:

- originality of thought
- ultimate benefit to the customer
- business potential
- quality improvement
- cost savings
- viability in implementation.

Three specific questions should be asked about each new idea:

1   Is it needed?

2   Is it practical?

3   Is it commercial?

Team innovation

New ideas and innovations often come from an individual but they are often only half-formed. These half-baked ideas should be developed by one or more others working as a team. This process is called 'team innovation' or 'team creativity'.

Team creativity should be encouraged in the innovative organisation. The natural, negative response to half-formed ideas should be pushed aside and a positive attitude to build on them encouraged. Attitudes should not be critical but positive and constructive.

Belbin identified nine team member roles:

1 **Plant:** solves difficult problems.
2 **Resource manager:** explores opportunities and develops contacts.
3 **Co-ordinator:** clarifies goals, promotes good decision-making and delegates effectively.
4 **Shaper:** has the drive and courage to overcome obstacles.
5 **Monitor/evaluator:** sees all options and judges them accurately.
6 **Team worker:** listens, is co-operative and diplomatic.
7 **Implementer:** turns ideas into practical actions.
8 **Completer:** tests for errors and omissions, and delivers on time.
9 **Specialist:** provides knowledge and skills in specialist areas.

A good team will exhibit all of the above 'roles', not necessarily with nine different people, but with fewer team members adopting different roles to complete the task.

Encouraging creativity in teams (besides helping individuals to 'perform' the Belbin roles within a team) depends on a manager's skills at:

- using the different skills within the team (having first identified the attributes of each individual)
- ensuring conflicts of ideas are allowed to happen and are tolerated by all
- recognising particularly good contributions

- helping the team generate ideas (e.g. by brain-storming)
- creating an open environment where individuals can speak up honestly.

Communicating about innovation

The good team leader will communicate effectively about progress, giving the team regular feedback as well as listening to their thoughts and ideas. Progress is a great motivator. The leader should:

- make regular opportunities to talk and listen to the team about progress and changes that are being made along the way.
- Explain why certain ideas have been implemented or chosen for further investigation and why others have been rejected at that time.
- Give recognition to those ideas that are developed and provide rewards to the people who generated them.

CHECKLIST FOR BUILDING ON IDEAS

- Do all the team members understand the problem?

  _____

- Do they focus together on each aspect of the problem?

  _____

- Do they work as a team building on each others ideas?

  _____

continued

CHECKLIST FOR BUILDING ON IDEAS continued

- Do they make sure everyone in the team understands each idea?

  _____

- Do they discuss things at a high enough level?

  _____

- Do they use analogies to develop ideas?

  _____

- Do the team listen to each other?

  _____

- Do the team members reserve criticism for an appropriate time?

  _____

- Do the team members improve on incomplete ideas?

  _____

- Do they completely explore an idea before dismissing it?

  _____

Brainstorming

In leading a brainstorming session the four main steps are:
1   Introduce the aim of the session
2   Warm-up if necessary by doing a practice exercise (eg. 20 uses for a hammer)
3   State the problem but don't be too detailed
4   Guide the participants by giving them time to think and generate ideas and then help them maintain a free-flow of ideas.

In leading a session which is 'sticky' and short of ideas to start with, ask 'what if ' questions to stimulate thought.

The rules of team brainstorming:
*   **There should be no judicial judgement:** A brainstorming session is not the place for criticism of ideas. All thoughts and ideas should be voiced, however outlandish they seem, as they may stimulate someone else to be creative.
*   **All crazy ideas should be welcomed:** It is easier to tone down a wild idea than it is to build one up.
*   **Quantity is wanted:** The more ideas that are generated, however ill-formed, the more likelihood there is of finding a good one.
*   **Idea combinations should be encouraged:** Team members should be invited to suggest how a colleague's idea could be developed, or how two or more ideas could be amalgamated.

Brainstorming sessions can often lead to a 'chain-reaction' between workers as ideas are developed openly. A small spark from one person can lead to many other ideas, building gradually into a great innovation.

The right climate will encourage the team to express ideas, however ill-formed. Creativity cannot be organised but some structures will encourage it. Communications should be positive and confident but also realistic and essentially constructive.

Brainstorming sessions should always be followed up, perhaps in smaller groups and ideas should then be evaluated by:

- deciding the selection criteria
- selecting obvious winning ideas
- eliminating the unworkable ideas
- sifting ideas into groupings and selecting the best in each
- applying the selection criteria to obvious winners and 'best of' the various groups
- testing the selections by 'reverse brainstorming' (i.e. in how many ways can this idea fail?)
- informing the participants of further developments.

Team training is important to improve team performance. Training to improve effective thinking and communication skills can really help a team to develop and work more efficiently together.

- Do you use brainstorming as a technique whenever the appropriate situation arises?

  _____

  _____

- Do your brainstorming sessions work and if not, do you know what you can do to improve them?

  _____

  _____

- Are you leading the sessions effectively?

  _____

  _____

- Have you considered appointing another member of the team to lead the session?

  _____

  _____

- Have you experimented with any variations on the basic brainstorming method?

  _____

  _____

- Can you think of examples of when brainstorming has generated good ideas and improved creative thinking in your organisation?

  _____

  _____

continued

- Do you and your organisation make use of creative thinking project groups and teams?

  _____

  _____

- Do you and your managers have a list of problems that could benefit from brainstorming?

  _____

  _____

Two more methods of collecting ideas

A leaders challenge is to elicit new ideas and thoughts from the workforce. Brainstorming is a good way to do this but two other proven methods are:

1   suggestion schemes; and
2   quality circles.

Lets look at each of these in turn.

Suggestion schemes

Suggestion schemes need enthusiastic support from top management for them to be successful. Management should ask specific, thought provoking questions to give people a direction for their thinking. A management team which is eager for innovation, expects ideas to be forthcoming and is determined to generate them is much more likely to have a successful suggestion scheme. Management should also give a quick response to all suggestions made, even if this is just a letter or a quick meeting to acknowledge receipt and to say the idea is being looked into in more depth.

It should be remembered that money is rarely the motivating factor in generating new ideas: recognition and a sense of achievement are usually far more important to the individual.

The drawback of suggestion schemes is that they don't adhere to the key principal of team creativity – they are highly individualistic. By contrast, Quality Circles do involve team creativity.

Quality circles

Quality circles involve a group of four to twelve people from the same work area or department voluntarily meeting to solve their work-related problems.

For quality circles to flourish they need:
- Top management commitment
- Members to voluntarily participate
- Members to be trained in teamwork
- Members to have a shared work background
- To be solution orientated
- Recognition and support from top management.

The main reason quality circles fail is because of lack of support from management. A commitment to provide training and resources on a long-term basis should come from all levels of management.

CHECKLIST FOR THE GENERATION OF IDEAS

- Is there an internal market for innovative ideas?

  _____

  _____

- Do teams allocate time to consider ideas?

  _____

  _____

- Do you and your teams spend time away from the office to review performance and plans?

  _____

  _____

- Are customers/suppliers involved in innovation in your business?

  _____

  _____

- Do you have successfully innovative teams and/or individuals and can you identify reasons for their success?

  _____

  _____

- Do you have a suggestion scheme that works?

  _____

  _____

- Are new ideas properly rewarded?

  _____

  _____

continued

- Do you help ensure ideas are not lost through poor presentation?

  _____

  _____

- Do you know of an alternative route to profitability and growth other than through innovation?

  _____

  _____

Dealing with change and overcoming obstacles to innovation

It is human nature to resist the unknown. Change, if it is very great or very sudden, can be alarming. We are more likely to respond to change in a positive way if it is gradual and expected. Innovation tends to mean a series of small changes over a period of time, a form of evolution within an organisation. This evolution needs to be carefully guided by leaders with personal and professional skills as well as enthusiasm.

Managers must ensure that creativity and innovation are not killed off by:
1   an initial response of outright condemnation, ridicule, rejection, damning criticism or faint praise
2   the vested interest of a particular person or department

3   too early an evaluation/judgement – sometimes
    suspending judgement early on can see an idea grow
    and reach a strong stage where it will work.

Criticism

Criticism has its place but should not be introduced too early
in the creative process. All relevant criticism should be
handled with tact and diplomacy, and explanations given
where necessary. Sometimes, challenging accepted views
and persisting in criticism, despite group pressures to
conform, may penetrate fixed ideas and create new ones.

Exercise: Overcoming obstacles

- Consider what obstacles exist in your organisation that may prevent individuals from
  putting ideas forward.
- Can you think of examples of when potentially
  good ideas have come to nothing because of
  these obstacles?

continued

Exercise: Overcoming obstacles continued

- Make a list of ideas for best practice which would allow the organisation to overcome these obstacles.

  _____

  _____

  _____

  _____

  _____

- Circulate your list to the managers in your organisation and discuss them further, and hopefully put them into action!

PART
THREE

Summary

A creative thinker and innovator in practice

The seven habits of successful creative thinkers
and innovators

Part three: Summary

A creative thinker and innovator in practice

In his autobiography, *Long After Sixty* (1975), Lord Roy Thompson of Fleet wrote:

> ❝ In my office I have always made myself accessible; I have always insisted upon this, to the extent often of not allowing my staff, or of not waiting for them, to vet strangers who came to see me before permitting them to come into my office. It is surprising the things that have sprung from this, the surprising things I have learned.

> I am always curious, always hopeful. I still often duck out of an office meeting to see what some visitor looks like and to find out what he wants. Likewise, I take quite a few telephone calls if my secretary happens to be busy or out of the room for the moment; I have told the switchboard that if there is not one of my personal staff to answer a call, to put it straight through to me. I don't want any information or opportunity to go elsewhere just because no-one could take a call.

I try to make friends wherever I go and it is my fond belief that I usually succeed. The way I look at it, everyone has an idea and one in a dozen may be a good idea. If you have to talk to a dozen people to get one good idea, even just the glimmering of an idea, that isn't wasteful work. People are continually passing things onto me, because I have given them to believe that I will be interested. Sometimes, usually when it is least expected, something comes up that is touched with gold. **"**

The seven habits of successful creative thinkers and innovators

1 Thinking outside the apparent confines of the problem/situation

- challenging the accepted
- ensuring you have defined the problem correctly
- not assuming existing practices, procedures or theories are absolutely correct
- widening your span of relevance by considering how other industries deal with similar problems.

Beyond the nine dots

Consider the puzzle below to discover how your mind works. Connect up the nine dots by using four straight lines without taking your pen or pencil off the paper. Allow yourself 3 minutes to solve the problem before turning to the Appendix on page 98 to find out the answer.

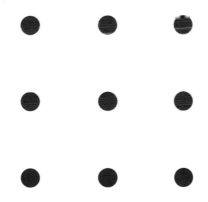

To be able to solve this puzzle you must challenge the assumption that the 'rules' mean that you should stay within the confines of the dots. Unconsciously imposing assumptions about a problem will put constraints on being able to find an answer.

We need to be able to think outside of the problem. We impose rules and frameworks around situations when we should be thinking more creatively than those boundaries allow. We need to have a wide span of relevance to be able to take our thinking outside the boundaries. We need to learn to 'leap over the wall' into what is the unknown and make it the known.

We should be aware of misconceptions, preconceptions and unconscious assumptions in our thinking. Listening to others when they challenge or test our assumptions may lead your ideas down a different, more beneficial path.

Making some assumptions deliberately and making connections between ideas that are apparently distant will involve a greater degree of creative thinking. This may help you explore ways forward but be aware not to commit yourself to these assumptions and make sure they are fully tested at a later date.

> 66 *Discovery consists of seeing what everyone has seen and thinking what nobody has thought.* 99
> Anon

CHECKLIST: BEYOND THE NINE DOTS

- Did you manage to solve the problem within the three minutes allowed?

_____

_____

- Are you able to appreciate the differences between unconscious and deliberately made assumptions?

_____

_____

- Are you aware of making untested assumptions?

_____

_____

- Are you able to find a balance between making imaginative assumptions and realistic assessments?

_____

_____

- Are you comfortable exploring options outside of the assumed boundaries?

_____

_____

- Are you able to evaluate your span of relevance and that of others?

_____

_____

continued

CHECKLIST: BEYOND THE NINE DOTS continued

- Do you find yourself blaming your lack of creativity on not having the correct specialist knowledge or education?

_____

_____

2   Welcoming chance intrusions

- being aware of the unexpected
- being open to chance.

Chance meetings or events can often provide the mind with creative food, providing the missing link in the solution to a problem. But, the creative thinker must be observant of everything around them in order to be aware of the chance and its meaning. This will open up many new ideas to you when you are not looking for them.

Having a wide span of attention and a broad range of interests will give you more opportunities to have chance meetings and experiences. Be open to the possibilities of transferring technology and ideas from one field to another. You will be more capable of this type of thinking if you have worked in more than one industry or have travelled abroad through your work.

Look out for chance meetings and events and don't wait for them to happen. Be sensitive and observant when interpreting these situations, realise their possible significance and add to them your own touch of creative thought.

CHECKLIST: CHANCE INTRUSIONS

- Can you recall seizing an opportunity because you were ready for it?

  _____

  _____

- Can you recall a chance event or meeting that aided some creative work you were undertaking?

  _____

  _____

- Are you observant of the happenings around you to be able to identify them as relevant to your creative thinking?

  _____

  _____

- Have you ever stumbled across opportunities when you weren't expecting them?

  _____

  _____

- Do you have a wide span of relevance which opens you up to more opportunities of chance meetings and events?

  _____

  _____

3 Listening to your depth mind (the unconscious mind)

- allowing your conscious mind the freedom to create
- sleeping on problems.

Creative thinking can be helped but it cannot be forced. If you are not making progress working on a problem sometimes it is best to put it aside and let your subconscious mind take over. Mental blocks can come from:

- **The lack of a starting point:** If the problem is so large it can be difficult to know where to start but jumping in usually provides some inspiration, even if it means beginning again at a different point.
- **A lack of perspective:** Sometimes you can be too close to a problem and therefore unable to see it clearly. Leaving it alone for a while can make it more approachable.
- **A lack of motivation:** Maybe you don't want to find a solution enough and have been put off your sense of purpose.
- **A lack of consultation with others:** Creative thinking should be a social activity to gain inspiration from others.

Allowing your mind to delve into its depths will allow you to develop new ideas and solutions not previously considered. Your depth mind is capable of analysing, synthesising and valuing at a subconscious level.

Sleeping on the problem often brings benefits. Your dreams, although not always directly relevant, can give you ideas and clues which will lead you to a solution. Sometimes you may not remember your dreams but they will come to you suddenly during the day. Some of our most valuable thoughts are those that come unsought.

Guidelines for improving the use of your depth mind:

- Practice makes perfect so use your depth mind as much as possible to innovate.
- See relationships between your thoughts and decisions despite their apparent differences of time, place and scale.
- Look at your mind as a sort of computer which holds lots of data and information. Allow your mind time to go through the sequences to piece together the information it holds to aid your creative process.
- Don't allow your mind to be lazy. Making your depth mind work for you can be hard work but if you persevere you will reap the benefits.

CHECKLIST: ARE YOU LISTENING TO YOUR DEPTH MIND?

- Are you aware that your depth mind can work productively for you, and are you willing to let it?

  _____
  _____

- Do you build time into your creative thinking to allow you to sleep on a problem?

  _____
  _____

- Do you consciously allow your depth mind to analyse complex problems, restructure theories and reach judgements?

  _____
  _____

- Do you recall experiencing a situation when your unconscious mind has solved a problem for you?

  _____
  _____

- Do you take note of and record your fleeting thoughts or half-formed ideas?

  _____
  _____

- Do you understand how your depth mind works and therefore how others work?

  _____
  _____

4   Suspending judgement

- not dismissing half-formed ideas prematurely
- only listening to creative critics.

Don't be too quick to criticise your own ideas or half-ideas, give them room to breathe and grow. They may just turn into something more productive. Also be aware that premature criticism from others can put a block on your creative thinking.

We should all be open to criticism from others if it is constructive and provided at the appropriate time during the creative process. This type of feedback is a way for us to improve ourselves and our ideas. Remember, two heads are often better than one.

It is useful to hear another person's perspective on a problem. They may have more experience or knowledge in that particular area, and they are likely to spot your unconscious assumptions and allow you to challenge your preconceptions.

CHECKLIST: SUSPENDING JUDGEMENT

- Do you tend to evaluate your own ideas or half-ideas too soon?

  _____

  _____

- Have you ever abandoned a promising idea because of someone's premature criticism?

  _____

  _____

- Can you think of situations when other people have had a positive impact on the development of your ideas?

  _____

  _____

- Do you know when and how to criticise others constructively?

  _____

  _____

5   Using the stepping stones of analogy

- looking at analogies in existing products and organisations
- making the familiar strange and the strange familiar.

Analogies can be a source of new ideas or new ways of approaching a problem. Many analogies come from situa tions in nature, where nature has evolved to solve a particular problem or necessity. Creative thinking often involves a leap in the dark to find something new. It often takes more than one step to reach the destination but if you can find an analogy of what the unknown idea might be like it will help you on your way.

Familiarity breeds conformity. We stop thinking about things we are over-familiar with. If we make the familiar unfamiliar it will give us a different perspective on the situation. Also, making the strange familiar can save you having to constantly reinvent when there is already a solution in existence.

Exercise: Putting the stepping stones of analogy into practice

- Identify a situation or problem in which you would like to try solving using an analogy.
  Next, think about analogies that are like the situation or problem you are trying to solve:

  1. _____
  2. _____
  3. _____
  4. _____
  5. _____

- Use these analogies to list the alternatives to your problem:

  1. _____
  2. _____
  3. _____
  4. _____
  5. _____

- Transfer these suggested solutions to the problem or situation in hand.

6 Tolerating ambiguity

- not jumping to certainties in the face of ambiguity
- allowing your depth mind time to work.

It can be easy to make a quick decision in the face of ambiguity and uncertainty but truly creative people are much more tolerant of being in a state of not knowing. They are better at overcoming and controlling the impulse to prematurely find a solution, which may be a good one but there is likely to be an even better one just around the corner.

Being in a state of not knowing can lead to stress and anxiety. To deal with those emotions, and not act prematurely, takes courage, perseverance and patience.

By being aware of your emotions you can make the decision to leave the problem for your depth mind to deal with for a while. Even then, when ideas start to emerge leave them alone for a while longer to develop themselves. Your detached interest will create the right climate for the seeds of ideas to grow.

CHECKLIST: TOLERATING AMBIGUITY

- Do you tend to whittle down your options to two decisions, the either/or, prematurely?

  _____

  _____

- Do people who cannot make decisions quickly irritate you, or do you have more patience?

  _____

  _____

- Can you think of three possible side-effects of living with uncertainty regarding a problem or situation?

  _____

  _____

- Are you able to switch off your stress and anxiety over a problem and leave it to your depth mind for a while?

  _____

  _____

- Do you show patience and perseverance in your work as a creative thinker?

  _____

  _____

- While in a state of uncertainty are you constantly looking for possible answers and connections to the solution?

  _____

  _____

7   **Banking all ideas from all sources**
  - sharpening curiosity and skills of observation
  - appreciating your surroundings and gathering inspiration from them.

The creative thinker and innovator should practice:
  - Being curious
  - Skills of observation
  - Listening
  - Reading
  - Travelling
  - Recording

By practicing these skills you will be committing informa-tion and knowledge to the depth mind for later use.

Curiosity is the basis for learning, an eager desire to know more is the stimulus for motivation. Ken Rowat writing in The Guardian, 1979 said:

> 66 *Creative activity, agonising though it may be at times, is essentially life enhancing, often joyful, and this can be judged not from the fixed smiles worn by models advertising power tools but by the extent to which the individual is seriously engrossed in his activity. Outside making love, men and women never feel better than when they are totally engaged in exploration or construction, especially when the motivation is simple: 'I wonder what will happen if I do this?'* 99

To be observant means to give careful, analytical attention to what you see. We miss so much of what is around us in everyday life because we don't really observe. It is good practice to really look at things; people, objects and scenes, as if you have never seen them before. Then record what you see so that the details are committed to memory; you never know when they might just be useful.

Be curious when you listen to things. Keep an open mind, don't be too analytical too quickly and use your judgement carefully about what you are hearing. Always make sure you fully understand what is being said to you. Ask questions to clarify if needs be. You cannot evaluate what you are listening to until you fully understand the meaning and intention behind it.

Reading is a great way to exercise the mind, to keep it active, open and eager to learn. Books hold untold amounts of information which, if removed from their setting, may make sense and have a connection to your present situation or problem. Reading fiction and poetry, as well as non-fiction, is a good way of stimulating and exercising the imagination.

Travelling gives you the opportunity to experience things you would not normally encounter, thereby adding to your bank of information and widening your horizons and thoughts. It also helps to make the familiar strange. If we did not venture beyond our own country we would not know how it differed from other cultures.

Recording your thoughts and observations is a very useful habit. It is a way of committing information to the mind for future reference. It also allows you to browse through your notes and play with new combinations and connections which might not normally have occurred to you.

CHECKLIST: BANKING IDEAS

- Think about how you could improve your curiosity.
- As a curious person, what five questions would you ask someone you had just met?
  1. _____
  2. _____
  3. _____
  4. _____
  5. _____

- Can you recall beneficial observations that have come from you being curious?
- Would you consider yourself a good listener?
- Do you use questions when listening to new ideas to make sure you fully understand them?
- Do you read books and articles to keep your mind stimulated?
- Do you read fiction to develop your imagination?
- Have you ever travelled as a means to finding new ideas related to your job?
- Do you choose holidays that stimulate and refresh both your mind and your body?

Conclusion

CHECKLIST FOR CREATIVITY AND INNOVATION

- Can you give an example of when you have used lateral thinking?

- Do you see problems as opportunities and maintain a positive attitude to them?

- Do you fear ridicule when you present a new idea to your colleagues?

- Are you very self critical?

- Do you make time to think clearly?

- Is your stress within manageable levels?

- Are you capable of challenging the accepted?

- Are you able to look further than the immediate logical answer?

- Are you able to inspire your staff to be creative?

---

continued

CHECKLIST FOR CREATIVITY AND INNOVATION continued

- Do you encourage creativity and innovation in teams as well as individuals?

- Is your organisation committed to innovation from the top?

- Is your organisation tolerant of failure?

- Is internal communication good at all levels?

- Are ideas generated from many different sources?

- Can you recall actual creative/innovative initiatives that have been put into practice in your organisation?

Innovation needs the generation, harvesting and imple-mentation of ideas. Managers good at innovation accept risk, are flexible and are motivated to take ideas through to completion.

How far you develop your skills as a creative thinker and innovator is largely down to you. Your level of motivation to succeed as a manager will play a big role in how high you set your goals. Remember, the future of our industry and our civilisation as a whole depends upon the creative flair and innovative genius of people like you.

The end result of successful creative thinking and innovation is:

Motivated team members

Satisfied customers

Profitable organisations

Appendix

Solutions to problems

Exercises in logical thinking, pages 20–23

1 Each barber must have cut the others hair, so the businessman chose the barber which had given his rival the better haircut.

2 The trains are travelling at 60mph and one at 40mph towards each other. Between them they will cover 100 miles in one hour. Therefore they will meet after one hour. The plane is flying backwards and forwards at 80mph. Therefore the plane is flying at 80mph for one hour. By re-arranging the relationships within this problem we can easily work out the answer.

3 Sandra carries the cat to the car and returns to the house empty handed.
Then Sandra carries Jennifer to the car and brings the cat back to the house.
Sandra then leaves the cat in the house while she carries Carl to the car. She then returns empty handed to the house and carries the cat to the car.

4 If the TV presenter walks Jane's dog, then Jane is not the TV presenter. The teacher taps on Louise's wall, indicating that Louise is not the teacher, therefore the teacher must be either Donna or Jane. But Jane cannot tap on Louise's wall because Donna is in the middle. So, Donna must be the teacher. Jane, since she is neither the TV presenter nor the teacher, must

be the nurse. Louise must therefore be the TV presenter.

Beyond the nine dots (page 77)

There are various solutions, here are two of them:

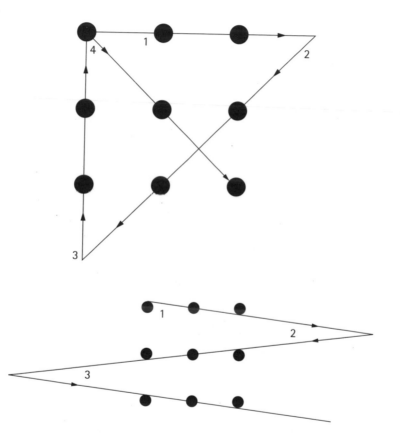

Quotes about creativity and innovation

'He that will not apply new remedies must accept new evils – for time is the greatest innovator.' Francis Bacon

'DARING IDEAS ARE LIKE CHESSMEN

moved forward.

THEY MAY BE BEATEN, BUT THEY MAY START A

winning game.' Goethe

'Experience has shown and a true philosophy will always show that a vast, perhaps the larger, portion of truth arises from the seemingly irrelevant.'
Edgar Allan Poe

'Discovery consists of seeing what everyone has seen and thinking what nobody has thought.'
Anon

'Thinking will always give you a reward, though not always what you expected.'
Roy Thomson

'In the case of the creative mind, it seems to me it is as if the intellect has withdrawn its guards from the gates. Ideas rush in pell mell and only then does it review and examine the multitude. You worthy critics, or whatever you may call yourselves, are ashamed or afraid of the momentary and passing madness found in all real creators... Hence your complaints of unfruitfulness — you reject too soon and discriminate too severely.'

Johann Schiller

'I invented nothing: I rediscover.' Rodin

'While the fisher sleeps, the net takes the fish.'

Old Greek Proverb

'A person would do well to carry a pencil in their pocket and write down the thoughts of the moment. Those that come unsought are commonly the most valuable and should be secured because they seldom return.'

Francis Bacon

'A new idea is delicate.
It can be killed by a sneer or a yawn:
it can be stabbed to death by a quip
and worried to death by a frown
on the right man's brow.'

Charles Brower

'God

HIDES THINGS FROM US BY PUTTING THEM CLOSE TO US'

Old saying

'Criticism often takes
from the tree caterpillars
and blossoms together.'
Old saying

*Don't be afraid of taking a big step – you
cannot cross a chasm in two steps.'*

David Lloyd-George

'A man without **patience** is a lamp without **oil.**'

Andres Segovia

'The mind connects things in unbelievable ways.'

George Benjamin

'One should never impose one's views on a problem; one should rather study it and in time a solution will reveal itself.'
Albert Einstein

'As soon as a thought darts, I write it down.'

Thomas Hobbes

'My chief job is to constantly stir or rekindle the curiosity of people that gets driven out by bureaucracy and formal schooling systems.'
Akio Morito

'There is a great deal of
unmapped country within us.'
English Proverb

'Curiosity is one of the permanent
and certain characteristics
of a vigorous intellect.' Samuel Johnson

'One doesn't discover new lands
without consenting to lose sight of the
shore for a very long time.' Andre Gide

'I question.'
Leonardo da Vinci's motto

'The disease of not listening.'

Shakespeare

'Many ideas grow better when transplanted
into another mind than in the one where
they sprung up.'
Oliver Wendell Holmes Jr

'Man never
rises to
great
truths
without
enthusiasm.'
Vauvenargues

'The typical eye
sees the ten per cent bad
of an idea and overlooks
the ninety per cent good.'

Charles F Kettering

'More creativity is the only
way to make tomorrow
better than today.'

Anon

The creative art thrives in an environment
of mutual stimulation, feedback and
constructive criticism – in a community of
creativity.'

William T Brady

'Chance favours only the prepared mind.' Louis Pasteur

**'Between the idea
And the reality…
Falls the Shadow.'**
T S Eliot

'Experience is the name we give our mistakes.'
Oscar Wilde

'An established company
which in an age demanding
innovation is not capable of
innovation is doomed to decline
and extinction. And a management
which in such a period does not
know how to manage innovation is
incompetent and unequal to its task.
Managing innovation will increasingly
become a challenge to management, and
especially top management, and a
touchstone of its competence.'

Peter Drucker

'The most important
of my discoveries have been
suggested to me by failures.'

Sir Humphrey Davy

Innovation is a gamble!

Sydney Brenner

'Without real commitment from the top, real innovation will be defeated again and again by the policies, procedures and rituals of almost any large organisation.'

Anon

There are costs and risks to a programme of action. But they are far less than the long-range risks and costs of comfortable inaction.' John F Kennedy

'The way to be safe is never to be secure.'

Benjamin Franklin

'What is honoured in a country will be cultivated there.'

Plato

'There is a natural opposition among men to anything they have not thought of themselves.'

Barnes Wallis

'People support what they help to create.'

Anon

'What's the secret of entrepreneurial success?
It's knowing when to use OPB (Other People's Brains)
and OPM (Other People's Money).'

J B Fugua

'Changing things is central to leadership. Changing them before anyone else is creativeness.'

Anon

'He that wrestles with us strengthens our nerves and sharpens our skill. Our antagonist is our helper.'
Edmund Burke

'He who dares nothing,
need hope for
nothing.'

English Proverb

Other Thorogood titles in this series

The Concise Adair on Leadership
Edited by Neil Thomas
£9.99 Paperback ISBN: 1 85418 218 8

Here in one short book is a practical master class in how to manage both yourself and others, to provide a team that is motivate, creative and high-performing. It encapsulates the essentials of Adair's writing on leadership and effective practice.

The Concise Time Management and Personal Development
By John Adair and Melanie Allen
£9.99 Paperback ISBN: 1 85418 223 4

This is both an expert and practical book to help you manage your time more effectively. It also shows you how to link daily action planning to the achievement of clearly identified long-term goals. It provides the tools, techniques and framework for continuing personal development and will prove invaluable in planning your own self-management as well as your career development.

The Concise Adair on Communication and Presentation Skills
Edited by Neil Thomas
£9.99 Paperback ISBN: 1 85418 228 5

Here in one book is everything you will ever need to know about good communication, presented by an acknowledged expert. This is an excellent introduction for anyone new to the subject and equally valuable as a constant refresher course for the more experienced. It covers: listening, reading skills, speaking and presentation skills, one-to-one interviews and managing meetings.

The Concise Guide to Telephone Tactics
By Graham Roberts-Phelps
£9.99 Paperback ISBN: 1 85418 278 1

Everything you will ever need to know about using the telephone in business by an expert sales trainer. It is divided into three sections: telephone tactics for customer satisfaction, gaining appointments and achieving better sales by telephone.

The Concise Adair on Team Building and Motivation
Edited by Neil Thomas
£9.99 Paperback ISBN: 1 85418 268 4

This book develops Adair's classic theory on Team, Task and Individual and summarises all his writing on leaders and motivation and getting the best from people. It includes sections on being motivated oneself, selecting people, target setting and reward and recognition.

Thorogood has an extensive range of books, professional insight reports and special briefings.

For a full listing of all Thorogood publications, or to order any title, call Thorogood Customer Services on 020 7749 4748 or fax on 020 7729 6110. Alternatively view our website on www.thorogood.ws.

Focused on developing your potential

Falconbury, the sister company to Thorogood publishing, brings together the leading experts from all areas of management and strategic development to provide you with a comprehensive portfolio of action-centred training and learning.

We understand everything managers and leaders need to be, know and do to succeed in today's commercial environment. Each product addresses a different technical or personal development need that will encourage growth and increase your potential for success.

- Practical public training programmes
- Tailored in-company training
- Coaching
- Mentoring
- Topical business seminars
- Trainer bureau/bank
- Adair Leadership Foundation

The most valuable resource in any organisation is its people; it is essential that you invest in the development of your management and leadership skills to ensure your team fulfil their potential.

Investment into both personal and professional development has been proven to provide an outstanding ROI through increased productivity in both you and your team. Ultimately leading to a dramatic impact on the bottom line.

With this in mind Falconbury have developed a comprehensive portfolio of training programmes to enable managers of all levels to develop their skills in leadership, communications, finance, people management, change management and all areas vital to achieving success in today's commercial environment.

WHAT FALCONBURY CAN OFFER YOU?

- Practical applied methodology with a proven results
- Extensive bank of experienced trainers
- Limited attendees to ensure one-to-one guidance
- Up to the minute thinking on management and leadership techniques
- Interactive training
- Balanced mix of theoretical and practical learning
- Learner-centred training
- Excellent cost/quality ratio

FALCONBURY IN-COMPANY TRAINING

Falconbury are aware that a public programme may not be the solution to leadership and management issues arising in your firm Involving only attendees from your organisation and tailoring the programme to focus on the current challenges you face individually and as a business may be more appropriate. With this in mind we have brought together our most motivated and forward thinking trainers to deliver tailored in-company programmes developed specifically around the needs within your organisation.

All our trainers have a practical commercial background and highly refined people skills. During the course of the programme they act as facilitator, trainer and mentor, adapting their style to ensure that each individual benefits equally from their knowledge to develop new skills.

Falconbury works with each organisation to develop a programme of training that fits your needs.

MENTORING AND COACHING

Developing and achieving your personal objectives in the workplace is becoming increasingly difficult in today's constantly changing environment. Additionally, as a manager or leader, you are responsible for guiding colleagues towards the realisation of their goals. Sometimes it is easy to lose focus on your short and long-term aims.

Falconbury's one-to-one coaching draws out individual potential by raising self-awareness and understanding, facilitating the learning and performance development that creates excellent managers and leaders. It builds renewed self-confidence and a strong sense of 'can-do' competence, contributing significant benefit to the organisation. Enabling you to focus your energy on developing your potential and that of your colleagues.

Mentoring involves formulating winning strategies, setting goals, monitoring achievements and motivating the whole team whilst achieving a much improved work life balance.

For more information contact Kate Jackson on:
+44 (0)20 7729 6677

Falconbury Business Seminars
10-12 Rivington Street, London EC2A 3DU, UK